Ted Rocne

Somefink in Particular

Poems and short sketches
recording the first months of our
Covid 19 Pandemic 2020

ISBN: 978-0-9935564-9-4

Published in the UK by:

Louannvee Publishing
www.louannveepublishing.co.uk

Dedicated to specialist nurse
Diana Backwell Moreira
and all her NHS colleagues

Acknowledgements

I should like to thank my wife Jill and our friends, in the White Cliffs Ramblers, for their encouragement despite being subjected to several of my poems. In addition I would like to thank my publisher: Louannvee Publishing, in particular Nettie, for the preparation of this book.

CONTENTS

I was told in late February of a local man, a retired scientist, who had barricaded himself and his wife in his house and stockpiled food.
Asked what I thought about it I said:
"Sounds like a crank."

Preface

This book reproduces thoughts and observations regarding the Covid 19 pandemic, recorded chronologically, over a five month period from March to August 2020. The first poem 'The Beginning' was written on 25th March following Lockdown and was shown to an online group of walking friends. Their encouragement prompted me to pen a few more until, after four months of following events with poems and sketches, it became apparent there was sufficient material for a publication. The book attempts to illustrate mainly, though not exclusively, the effects of this pandemic on peoples lives and behaviour and how they respond to an exceptional set of circumstances. Readers might know that previous books were entitled *Nuffink in Particular* so, for obvious reasons this book is called *Somefink in Particular.*

The Beginning

It could be a day like any other
but it isn't.
Everyone knows there's a shadow,
a dark, giant, sinister, evil shadow and
everyone knows it's moving.
Moving slowly, moving cumbersomely,
moving silently, relentlessly, lumbering toward us.
There's no roar, no growl, nothing to see,
nothing to hear but it's there.
Out there somewhere. We can feel it.
Looking for a host, to infiltrate, to carry, to incubate
and then to destroy.
Everyone knows.

But wait,
Looking out the window
It's a beautiful day!
The sun's shining, buds are opening,
birds are singing, birds are nesting,
looking for a mate, building for the future.
The seafront's crowded.
Full of dog walkers, joggers, cyclists,
working from homers not working from home,
and even the supposedly self isolating,
self hibernating 'at risk' elderly
all enjoying the sunshine.

And outside the café with 'Armageddon' lattes,
'end of the world' toasted tea cakes,
Cranberry and Brie 'apocalyptic' filled paninis and
'we're all doomed' salted caramel ice creams.
All perfectly normal.
A rude, impatient 'I'm in a hurry' man at
the cash machine and from his car window a man
shouting abuse at a woman trying to cross the road.
All perfectly normal.

But underneath,
underlying
there is awareness.
Everyone does know
and
panic buying says so.

Shape of things to come

1st Man: I'll swap you two rashers of bacon for a toilet roll.
2nd Man: You must be joking?
1st Man: Alright, two rashers of bacon and a bar of soap?
2nd Man: Try again.
1st Man: Two rashers of bacon, a bar of soap and sausage?
2nd Man: Done.

High Risk 1

She said: Could you sweep up those leaves out front?
He said: No sorry, I'm an elderly gentleman classified as 'at risk'!
She said: You don't have to go into the road. You can stay in the garden, well away from the road.
He said: No, no sorry too risky. You'll have to do it.
She said: Well I'm an elderly lady 'at risk'
He said: Yes, but you're not at risk as much as I'm at risk. So, the burden must fall on those least at risk. Rotten luck but there it is.
She said: So where are you going?
He said: Upstairs to read my poetry book. Self-isolation, following government guidelines.

NB Of course this is all fantasy. I swept up the leaves.

One Week Later

- Social Distancing -

Sitting on the seafront on my own bench,
looking out, through a heat haze,
at isolating tankers. Seemingly motionless
but moving.

Nearby a lady on her own bench,
there's no acknowledgement one to the other.
We both sit wrapped in confined surrealism
and both quite peaceful.

People are gliding round each other
giving more than two meters.
Avoiding each other.
Avoiding a sneeze or a cough.

A disabled man on a tricycle, trying
to open a gate, refuses help.
"It's alright thank you I can manage."
And he does. Somehow.

People do seem to be taking more notice.

Today I think there is hope.

Differing Opinions

"I'm sure when you passed that woman the gap was less than two meters and where's your sanitising lotion?"
Or
" Coronavirus!! Don't talk to me about coronavirus. I'm not having anyone telling me what to do!!"

Science Fiction

Producer: OK Murry what have you got for me?
Director: Hermann's come up with a good script for a Sci-fi movie
Producer: OK hit me with it.
Director: Well it's about this organisation that pays no attention to any other sucker and lets loose a terrible disease that gradually spreads from one country to another until thousands of people are going down the Swanee all over the world. People panicking. The whole works!
Producer: So, who's the hero. There must be a hero?
Director: A guy who's in a race against time to knock out a vaccine and save millions of people.
Producer: Too far-fetched. Try for something a bit more realistic. More human interest and less fiction.

Guess Who? Quiz

1st Man: The other day I heard a well known politician say the Coronavirus was nothing to worry about. The biggest hoax in history. People should get back to work.

2nd Man: That's a tough one. Give me another clue?

1st Man: He thinks the answer might be to drink bleach.

2nd Man: Really! Go on, another clue?

1st Man: He also said global warming's a load of rubbish.

2nd Man: Um, a member of the 'Flat Earth Society'?

1st Man: Close enough!

Or...

1st Man: I heard the other day a politician say: " We're gonna send this Coronavirus packing"

2nd Man: Oh, I know he also said: "We'll fight it in the street's and on the beaches, in the supermarkets and in the fields. We'll never surrender."

1st Man: Are you by any chance getting a bit confused with another politician?

2nd Man: No, I don't think so. Oh well perhaps I am getting a bit muddled. I thought for a moment I heard another voice. You'll have to give me another clue.

Two Weeks Later

Out for a walk this afternoon
One observes
The world, his wife and children exercising
Working from homers are now
Walkers from homers
Cyclists from homers
Joggers from homers
Plus, children from schoolers
Every day's a Sunday.

But
One also observes
People still weaving round each other
Still following the rules.
Still social distancing.
And if I'm out why shouldn't they be?

However
One further observes.
So many cars now back on the road.
All making 'essential journeys'?
All going to supermarkets?

An election slogan once said:
"Trust the People"
There must be a ? over this
Sometimes.

The Dentist

She said: I've just walked past the dentist and she's gone into lockdown.
He said: So, what do you think?
She said: I think it's not a good time to have a tooth ache.

The Telephone

She said: Your nephew's on the phone.
He said: Oh no!
She said: You'll have to talk to him. It's no good me pretending you're out.

Online Deliveries

He said: Have you been checking the supermarket online delivery service?
She said: Yes, all the slots are booked up for weeks and the site is shut down at present.
He said: Well I suppose they must be swamped at the moment. It can't all run smoothly.
She said: No, I can understand that. I just wish they wouldn't pretend it is!

Hawkshill

Up on Hawkshill, a beautiful morning.
Sitting on Charles seat and looking out to sea. `
A soporific, peaceful, blank canvass.
Looking out on a scene bathed, a scene wrapped,
a scene folded in comfortable embracing silence.
There's a chill wind but also a warm penetrating
sun so there is balance. A good exchange.

One watches the odd bird skimming across the landscape
and behind there's a sudden eruption of spring song.
So enchanting one thinks a blackbird and probably a nest
nearby but it needs conformation. Not that it really matters.
The sound's enough.

Somewhere in the distance one can hear a saw and
in the warm sunshine sleep would seem an easy, enticing,
option but now someone's approaching and social
distancing says it's time to move on.

Modern Technology

She said: The book club might keep going on 'on the web'
He said: That's a good idea.
She said: Yes but if they're not coming round I won't need to make any more cakes.
He said: What!! Oh no. I don't think that's a good idea.
She said: Why not?
He said: Well er… well because you need to keep practising.
It's like a bit of machinery. You have to keep it oiled to stop it going rusty.
She said: I see.
He said: Also. it's important to keep up morale. Especially for those at risk. Cake making 's all part of it.

The Queue

1st Elderly lady: You're nearly at the front of the queue.
2nd Elderly lady: Yes, that's right dear won't be long now.
1st Elderly Lady: Good idea having a special time for the elderly.
2nd Elderly lady: Yes it is.
1st Elderly Lady: And you're keeping two meters apart.
2nd Elderly lady: Yes, that as well. It's safer.
1st Elderly Lady: Well I'd better get to the back of the queue. Cheerio.
2nd Elderly Lady: Yes cheerio. Oh, not that way dear. You'll need to catch a bus to the end of the queue! There's one in a couple of minutes so you'll have to be quick. It's in that direction. Oh, but you mustn't sit near anyone. Keep the two meters...

New Dawn?

It maybe that within the folds of this cold
egregious wind that's blowing obdurately,
menacingly, searchingly across us
there are, possible, penetrating rays of hope.
Compassionate and sanguine rays of hope.
An elderly, almost centenarian, man has
touched the hearts of many, walking mile after
mile and on a more specific, closer to home
level people are seeking out others to shop,
to help, to assist, care for, look out for.
To realise humanity.

So perhaps barriers are being pierced a bit?
1940 reinvented a bit?
Perhaps the many years of 'every man for himself'
lifted a bit, prised open a bit?

But perhaps, on the other hand,
the undercurrent is still strong, still resistant,
and perhaps this is just a 'brief interlude,'
a 'shaft of light', ' a 'limited edition,'
'undercoat without gloss.'

Who knows?
We'll see.

The Queen's Speech

He said: Let's have a look in the paper. See what's on TV.

She said: The Queen's is making her speech tonight on TV.

He said: Yes, I know and I know what she's gonna say.

She said: How do you know?

He said: It was on TV this morning. The reporter told us what she'd say.

She said: Really?

He said: Yeah, so I'll see what else is on.

The Seat of Power

1st Man: I see we've got Dominic involved now. He'll soon sort things out.

2nd Man: You think so?

1st Man: Oh yes. He'll know how to deal with all these medical and scientific experts. See through all their mumbo jumbo.

2nd Man: You're sure about that?

1st Man: Yes, of course. He's a very clever chap. Got a 1st at Oxford in Ancient History! They won't know what to make of him or what he's talking about.

The Experts

He said: It seems this Coronavirus problem is going on for some time. Until May or June then it will tail off and then another month or so and we'll have a vaccine.

She said: How do you know?

He said: An expert on TV. A virologist from the university of Abu Dhabi said so.

She said: Really, well the expert I heard said that according to his model it could all go on for at least another year and the same goes for finding a vaccine. He showed all these statistics and graphs.

He said: No, that's not likely. According to my man's model everything will be back to normal by then. He had lots of statistics and graphs as well.

She said: No, no, my expert said that according to his model there could be a second wave.

He said: That's rubbish. Where did he come from?

She said: The faculty of Applied science Northampton Poly, so he should know.

Hot Cross Buns

He said: With the baker closed I've decided to make our own hot cross buns!

She said: Are you sure about this.

He said: Yeah of course I am. Just follow the recipe. Easy peasy.

Later…

She said: Never mind we'll keep them to defend ourselves in case of burglars.

Statistics

It should be the cricket season now
stretched out into the warmth of summer.
A trip booked to Headingley. Yorkshire v Kent.
Cream teas and lazy, dozing, days in the sun.
A routine followed in time. In our time.
In our concrete.

But now,
there's a different opponent.
A much more aggressive opponent.
Playing by its own rules and claiming as victims,
not runs but people.
People in the hundreds; people in the thousands.

In fact…
So many faceless victims we're only looking at
the scorecard. Just detaching the total.
So many names. So many people.
We can't personalise.

And there's a queue with more waiting.
Waiting for tomorrow and the day after that
and some still around this week but not next week.
Some waiting for the week after that
or the week after that.

At the moment,
it's only the scorecard,
only the numbers,
only statistics that matter.

Her Job

I get up every morning and wonder
what to have for breakfast.
A friend's daughter, a frontline nurse
in London, is being trained to deal
with people dying in numbers.
It's her job
it's her vocation.
So, every morning
I wonder what to have for breakfast
while
she watches people die.

In the Garden

He said: You see that pigeon over there. He doesn't have to worry about self isolation.
She said: No I suppose not.
He said: Goes where he likes
She said: It might be a she?
He said: OK goes where he or she likes. And look at his or her head.
She said: What about it?
He said: Never stops moving. Look twitch, twitch, twitch.
She said: So?
He said: Well. It's flexible. So he or she doesn't have to worry about arthritis or joining a 'virtual' pilates class.
She said: No I suppose not.

Desperate Times

He said: Have you noticed I've rubbed down and re-varnished the wooden lavatory seat in the downstairs toilet?
She said: Yes it looks very nice. You've done a good job.
He said: Have you tried it yet?
She said: No... no, I'm saving it up. Something to look forward to.

New Routine

There now seems to be a new routine where
self isolation can mean less isolation.
The constraints of calendar, or the straight jacket of
timetable, seem to have loosened and spawned a new,
often imaginative, often innovative routine.
Perhaps a routine procreated by necessity.
Days merge into other days. Days blended into other days
and there's a great vortex of time to consume.
A great vacant space to be filled.
Differently.

For Many
it's being filled by communication.
By bucket and bucket loads of communication.
No longer simmering along in the old interrupted hesitant
containers of time but now constantly on the boil.
Bubbling, bubbling away with shovel loads of emails,
virtual, online meetings, social networking apps,
and so on and so on. All poured into the giant IT
pot to keep it constantly topped up and on the boil.
It's a tsunami of communication.
For others the road to Nirvana is lined with pot holes; travel
only for the initiated. For the IT literati. For the IT savvy.
For some it's a lunar landscape, never to be reached.
Never to be lived in.

For many
there's vortex filling conversation.
Not 'computer screen conversation' but live. A live,
social distancing show on the streets, talking and talking,
in the sunshine, every day. Like wartime.
Like the replicated tales of 1940's mum.

"Did you hear there's flour down the road in the farm shop?"
"And did you know there's pasta in the health food shop?"
"No, crikey, better get down there before it's all gone."
Also, on the global level,
"Where's it all going to end, that's what I'd like to know."
"Search me. I don't think they know themselves."
A routine of less isolation at more than two meters.

And for many
it's a routine of exercise.
An endless stream of walkers, joggers, cyclists,
as if suddenly released from years of solitary confinement.
All weaving their social distancing ways along.
Sliding in, sliding out, this way, that way, your dog,
my dog, stopping, chatting, back to weaving, back to chatting,
same again tomorrow.
And so many pensioners all training for an imaginary
Olympics and bags full of gold. Confident of survival.

And finally, there's the DIY filler.
Unrestrained activity in the garden and buildings restored
and jobs sitting in the 'in tray' marked 'moribund'
decaying for years, now being tackled with bionic zest,
enthusiasm, dormant for years.
And all spawned from boredom and necessity.
There's a new routine.

PS For many of the elderly, lonely, already isolated,
non-savvy, financially poor, spiritually poor, living in large
towns on large housing estates with little or no green spaces,
delete or disregard much, or all, of the above.

Doing What's Best

He said:	You've just eaten that whole giant bag of crisps.
She said:	Yes I know. I came over a bit peckish. I've Saved you a few. Well, not very many.
He said:	Oh that's good. Thanks.
She said:	Yes but on second thoughts I'll have to eat them.
He said:	Really!
She said:	Yes. They're not good for your gums or your stomach.
He said:	No I suppose not.
She said:	And you're an elderly man at risk so I'll have to finish them. It's for your own good.

Deprivation

She said:	I've bought you a bar of chocolate
He said:	Oh goody.
She said:	Yes your favourite, plain chocolate.
He said:	Oh good!
She said:	Yes but you can't have it.
He said:	Oh! Can't I?
She said:	No it's in quarantine.
He said:	Oh I see. Can I sit and look at it?
She said:	Yes I think that'll be alright but don't get too close.

Nostalgic Pond

One feels we've been diving into and swimming
around in, a giant nostalgic pond for weeks now.
Swirling around in 'Dunkirk spirit,' 'backs to the
wall' and if 'we all stick together' we'll send this
corona virus 'packing.' 'By jingo we will.'

Yesterday was VE Day but swimming around
and peering through the pond's murky memories
I've already seen Jack Hawkins still trying to sink
those beastly U Boats; Celia Johnson and Robert
Newton, still trying to keep the family together
Leo Glen still lugging the wooden horse around
Stalag Luft 111 and John Mills who seemed to be
in all the films; in the Army, in the Navy and in
the Air force, almost all at the same time.

Of course Churchill's everywhere! The war leader,
the politician, the painter. I've seen him many times;
reviewing troops, during the blitz, giving speeches.
And King George V1 and Queen Elizabeth;
growing up, in the army, driving trucks.
And the old faithful war series of yesteryear
They've all been in the pond; not
difficult to find for weeks now.

And what of the swimmers?
Many of those still within reach, chronologically,
enjoy the pond. Love wallowing, floating around
in the warm, soft, comfortable memories.
But looking around there are younger swimmers
here as well. Perhaps more to do with curiosity
than familiarity but here all the same.

In the end I fasten onto Celia Johnson, care worn,
in pinny, with arms folded, who might be saying:
"What's going to become of us all? That's what
I'd like to know. Answer me that."

The Cavalry

Dear Diary

Over the hill the cavalry arrived today
bringing much needed sustenance and victuals
to us, the poor beleaguered settlers.
The captain, a friendly sort of feller, a mite long
in the tooth, also brought news of the plague hereabouts
and said he'd been into Dealsville.

Well, he was real riled up and said he was mighty
sorry to see so many townsfolk and so many buggies and
so many young'uns all over main street and up and down the
side streets and them not giving a hoot or a holler for
all the signs pinned up about the plague. Telling them:
"You all must stay indoors and you all must stay put."
He said most of the stores were shut, excepting
the general provision store but it made not a
lick of difference to all 'them folk' and their
young'uns which was a going around every which way.

Course I asked him about the law but he said the
sheriff was no where's to be seen. Maybe
holed up in his office or locked himself into one of his
own jails. The folks was doing as they pleased and
Lord knows no-one was taking a blind bit of notice.
Well, I thought long and hard and in the end
I came to the conclusion:
"There's something cock-eyed somewhere."

Equal Rights

To whom it may concern.

It has been noted and remarked on, by some, that
since the lockdown it's my poor, long suffering wife,
who's been constantly engaged in tasks normally
described as Do It Yourself.
For example the restoration of our front porch,
garden room and many other worthy projects.
In fact she's rarely seen without a pot of paint.

I should now, therefore, like to take this opportunity
to point out, to those of a sceptical and uncharitable
disposition, that as a long time supporter of the
women's movement and equal rights, which includes
the right to paint and decorate, I have consciously
decided, on this occasion, not to interfere and
reluctantly, to adopt a more 'drone' like posture for
the duration of this confinement.
I am, of course, at the same time, always keeping
myself available for consultation.

Yours Faithfully

E Roche (equal opportunities husband)

PS I also take comfort in the knowledge that she never looks
at social media

Down on the Coast

There is a sense of being a spectator who's peering
through a window of events unfolding elsewhere.
Unpicking reality in an episodic drama of unreality.
A sense in which it seems like a story that's about
other people in other places. Not about us.

People in cities, on housing estates, hospitals,
care homes. All seemingly distant from us.
They appear as the people cast in the lead roles and
unless we know any of them, we sit and watch.
The audience. Partially detached.

Of course, we still maintain the two meters and clap on
Thursdays which keeps a thread, keeps a feeling of
belonging, but then we put the kettle on and watch a
program about house prices or life in ancient Rome.

Evacuated to north Devon, during the Blitz, my mother
recounted a similar drama.
Of course, not the same communication, only radio and still
many gas lamps and stone floors but the same detachment,
the same removal - almost inconvenience, of life disrupted
by:
people with different accents and different lifestyles.
People fleeing bombs.

The news gives a window but we can only travel so far and
distance gives protection.
Or so it appears.

Easing Restrictions

Guidelines given liberally
may well be
interpreted liberally.

Tough Decisions

The small incursion of a stone onto the front
windscreen of my wife's car has seen a crack
gradually travelling and creating a path towards
the opposite side.
Difficulties in arranging its replacement has
led to the requisitioning of my vehicle.
The raison d'etre:
In times of emergency we must all make
sacrifices in the interests of others. Decisions
are made for the common good.

(pause…)

"And you're not using it anyway."

PS When the man finally came to replace the window

He said:

"After two months furlough and
after twenty-six years in the job,
I don't want to do it anymore."

To do or not to do

To wear a mask or not to wear a mask
That is the question.
To go for a walk and just walk or to sit, or to sunbathe
That is the question.
To meet one person, who is not related, but not two people
Or to meet two people who are related
That is the question.
To meet one person out front, keeping two meters
Or to meet them in the garden, keeping two meters.
That is the question
To stay with the small shops or start using the supermarkets
That is the question.
To stay at home and isolate or...
                    drive two hundred miles to Durham
That is the question.
And all these questions while trying to 'stay alert'
And figure out what day it is.
There's the question
And there's the rub!

Plagues

The Black Death 1348

A great bubonic banquet hosted by rats and fleas
with a compulsory, open invitation, to many thousands.
No need to reply. Informal dress and times may vary
for a fixed, limited menu.
And attend they did in their thousands
because they knew nothing
and were helpless.

The Great Plague 1665

Another bubonic feast attended by many thousands
and this time with rhyming accompaniment
"Ring a ring of roses
a pocket full of posies
atishoo, atishoo we all fall down"
And they did in their thousands
because they knew nothing
and were helpless.

Spanish Flu 1918

Nothing to do with rats or fleas or Spain but 'virus
hosted' with Americans as the first guests.
Then so many invites sent out to millions waiting
patiently all over the world.
And attend they did
because they knew very little
and were helpless.

Covid 19 2020

And now a virus hosted, pandemic banquet, by
curtesy of China.
Invitations to attend by contact, by touch, by sneeze
or cough sent out to thousands.
And thousands attend
because now they know everything
but are still, more or less, helpless.

Covid 19. A Consequence?

In Greek mythology Hermes worked for the Gods.
Fleet of foot, swiftly and freely moving around the
globe aided by his winged sandals. He was the herald.
He did the work. He met the demand.

Now, much the same, there is the 'online delivery' deity.
A supreme being already established, already claiming
territory but now growing more and more fat from
gorging on weeks and weeks of coronavirus.

His ubiquitous emissaries online logistics 'experts'
and leading supermarkets
and a host of other loyal and devoted acolytes serve
their master faithfully and engage their own heralds
to travel the land, to meet demand.
No need for 'winged sandals,' the online delivery herald
has his van and no need for Divine guidance. The herald
has his post codes, satnavs, and smart phones.

Even before lockdown one muses on the mummified department stores, festering, closing down, boarded up and evoking memories of shipyards, steel yards and steam trains all shunted remorselessly, inevitably, pre-programmed, into the endless graveyard of history.

Does it matter? No not really!
Only in the cobwebs of memory as another key in the life of social beings to linger, wander, engage and gossip away - the clock is turned.

Experts - II

The expert sits woven into his web of knowledge. Gathered, accumulated, layer by layer, stored and sorted over years and years of patient, painstaking, single minded devotion.
And it's exclusive, privatised knowledge, available only to the few. To those who trod the path.
Not available, not easily accessible and shrouded in obdurate, unyielding mystery for the many.

Around him the expert collects an aura. He is the omniscient arbiter of truth and certainty to be handed down. To be dispensed on request with prescriptions of what to do, what measures to take, what's to be to implemented, enforced if necessary, in order to secure salvation.
The predictive tablets of truth and certainty to be taken and digested as prescribed.

So far so good.
But now there are other experts and they have also gathered and accumulated, over many years of devotion, their own web of knowledge and they are writing out different prescriptions for different medications of truth and certainty. Also to be taken and digested as prescribed.

Outside the caves of experts the many sit confused and disorientated and try to decide which expert is the real harbinger, the real keeper of enlightenment, the real deity to give truth and certainty.

The experts are necessary. The people need experts but don't expect experts and perfection.

Relations

"Just because we're related don't run away with the
idea you're coming into my bubble.
I'm drawing up a short list."
"Right well if that's the way you feel. Two can play
at that game. I'll start up my own bubble."
"That's fine by me. You stay in your bubble
and I'll stay in mine."

Easing Down

Gradually the shadow seems to be lifting
The shroud of gloom less pressing, less penetrating.
And looking out from the bedroom window the
sun still shines but now more relaxed, not the
same anxiety, not the same alarm.

The doors of old routines are beginning to open,
creeping open, thin shards of light are seeping in,
for people to plan, people to meet,
the numbers increasing, the prospects expanding.

But caution,
the shadow's still there, still hovers, still lingers,
waiting, biding its time to expand, to consume.
To re-energize.

There is cause for optimism.
Tempered optimism.

No Mystery

She said: I thought you were supposed to be taking Biffo
For a walk?
He said: That's right I did take him for a walk.
She said: What, all this time?
He said: We went for a long walk.
She said: You've been round Jim's drinking beer and
watching the football.
He said: What makes you think that?

She said: Because you've been sucking mints to try to hide the smell but you made a mistake because you should have given one to Biffo. He's been drinking beer and eating crisps as well; there's bits round his collar. And I happen to know it was West Ham's game on the telly so that clinched it.

He said: I suppose you think you're clever?

She said: Not really. It's called 'track and trace' but I didn't need an app.

Crossroads

And now as we sink snugly into our duvets of Covid
complacency, more relaxed, more confident, some
experts still say 'with certainty' that the shadow waits,
just off stage, peeking round the corner, getting ready
to make a grand re-appearance, perhaps in the autumn,
to enter stage left, with a fanfare, stronger than ever.
Once again seeking out, stalking, absorbing.
But...
Other experts say the economy groans under its straight
jacket of idleness. Screams to be released. Demands to be
released for the comfort and security of the many.
Our stocks of coal to keep the home fires burning are,
it seems, running dangerously low.
So...
Shops are opening, hairdressers, pubs, restaurants, small
gatherings, keeping one meter, all mingling into their
supposedly tight fitting, changing bubbles.

The Covid scales are finely balanced,
weighted at one end with lives,
at the other end with jobs.

An Appointment

1st Lady: So when I got there, there was this woman wearing a mask and visor, one of those all in one suits. I had to have my temperature taken and wear a mask. Towels were being washed and sanitized and they were only letting three people in at a time.

2nd Lady: Well you can understand. That's the way they have to be in the hospitals. Wearing all the gear. They can't be too careful!

1st Lady: Who's talking about hospitals? I'm talking about going to the hairdresser.

Idle Moment

Early morning.
Looking through the window, through the rain
in an idle Covid moment, at sparrows feeding from
their drenched overhanging bird feeder.
There's pushing and shoving to get on the perch
and the strongest and fittest are winning the day.
Females with babies are holding their own but
only just and for the rest, not much to spare.
It's bullies in action. It's Darwin in action.
There's no place here for the weak.
No refuge, no future, no salvation,
without intervention.

Good News

The main danger has passed and our shadow of evil
is in decline, in retreat, on the run.
So said a professor, in so many words, this morning.
Why?
Because now we know his strategy, his modus operandi,
he can no longer sneak up on us and
where ever he launches an attack we'll be ready.
Ready with a salvo of test and trace and if
necessary another period of confinement.
So good news.
But…
What of our people after liberty restored?
'Can we get them back on the farm
 after they've seen Paris?'
'Can we shove grumpy genie's back into bottles?'

Another imponderable!!

Medication

Doctor:	Ah Mr English. Do come in. What can I do for you?
Mr English:	It's these new tablets doctor. After years of taking the austerity tablets I'm a bit confused.
Doctor:	Really?
Mr English:	Yes these new spending tablets take a bit of getting use to. Bit of a shock to the system. What's the idea?
Doctor:	Well it's all part of the plan to get you back on your feet again Mr English. Build you up. Get you ready for the future.
Mr English:	Is that because the austerity tablets weren't working then doctor?
Doctor:	No, no, no, we're just trying out a different medication. That's all.
Mr English:	I see. Only I've got a friend in Germany who's been taking the spending tablets for a long time and he seems to be in much better shape than I am?
Doctor:	Really? Oh no I don't think so. I wouldn't put too much store by that!

All Change

She said: Are you going down the shop?
He said: Yes I am.
She said: Well don't forget to wear your mask.
He said: I thought they weren't sure about that?
She said: No, no that's all changed. They're saying we must wear masks now in shops and when travelling.
He said: I wish they'd make up their minds.
She said: I think we'll have to cancel the restaurant as well.
He said: But they've only just reopened and they're giving people ten pounds to go...
She said: I know but there's public in there as well isn't there?
He said: Yes I know but aren't they having to sit sideways and anyway you could always wear your mask.
She said: How can I eat with a mask on?
He said: Well you could lift your mask up when you put your food in.
She said: Like an oyster you mean?
He said: Yeah that's it. Mask up, food in, mask down, close mouth. Simple. All very straightforward.
(pause)
She said: What about getting some fish and chips?

Financial Issues

◊◊◊ On the Bread Line ◊◊◊

She said: They just said on the news that the owner of a 'most used, most popular' online delivery service has seen his personal income increase by thirteen billion in one day.

He said: Is that dollars or pounds?

She said: Dollars probably. Does it matter?

He said: Oh yes there is a difference. It could be a worry for him if he didn't know.

◊◊◊ What's Money? ◊◊◊

He said: They just said on the news that the EU has set up a 750 billion euro Covid reconstruction fund. A loan not a rebate.

She said: So what does that mean?

He said: I think it means the Germans and French may have just taken out a 750 billion euro loan.

NB My wife says on this planet there are worlds within worlds.

Trouble in the Aisles

He came towards me pushing his trolley,
a lady by his side.
A bit unkempt, mid-forties, medium height,
medium build, giving me, it seemed, 'the once over.'
I moved to one side to allow him to pass,
but as we came together, he suddenly said,
rather aggressively:
"Oi, don't you know you're walking the wrong way,
this is one way only."
"Oh, really?" I replied, rather taken aback, but as
fortune would have it, at that moment, a female
member of staff appeared and said: "No he
isn't. This aisle is both ways."
To his credit the man replied: "I apologise,"
and moved on. So no harm done.
But one couldn't help but conjecture that
had I been a champion heavyweight lookalike, he
might not have said anything.

‘On the Web’

The poetry group’s first virtual venture.
Everything’s ready.
Practice completed, trial runs undertaken.
All is in place. Fair stands the wind as
I sit looking at the screen.
Two minutes to go, tension increasing.
One minute to go, anxiety mounts.
Counting down the seconds.
Five, four, three, two, one and 'lift off'
‘NOW’ is displayed and it’s all systems go.
We’re off. We’re off. We’re off.

Except, that we’re not.
There’s just me on the screen, looking at me,
looking back at me, looking bewildered.
“Press ‘Gallery View,’” says my wife, “that might open
it up and let the others in.”
But there is no ‘Gallery View’ just a row of
other options and no handy six-year-old to give
tuition and tell me which one to click.

So I try this one, try that one, try everyone
and now we’re back to ‘Home Page’ and
a notice advising me my guests are in the
‘waiting room’ waiting to come in.
“Well tell them to come in,” I shout at the laptop,
“and what have you done with my ‘Gallery View’?
You've hidden it somewhere! Where have you put it?”

Events now go from bad to worse as my wife,
light years ahead of me on the IT front,
jumps ship and is off to the hairdressers.
Passing through the front door with a regretful
but cheery: "Sorry got to go. Good Luck."

It's the final straw, left alone, bereft,
IT Special Needs, no relief in sight, the games up.

But then...
Never say die, over the hill, via the telephone,
comes the cavalry in the form of Nettie B,
one of our younger members (in fact our only
younger member) she suggests we abandon the
first stage and regroup for the second scheduled meeting.

So...
It's situation saved but I'm wiped out for the rest
of the day with stress, relieved, only partially,
late afternoon by England winning the test match.

Japan

It seems that in Japan,
despite a population of over a hundred and twenty million,
only nine hundred people have died of Covid 19.

And it seems that non tactile modes of greeting and
natural self distancing might have played a part.

And it seems that the previous habitual wearing
of face masks might have played a part.

And it seems that great respect and high regard
for the elderly in Japanese society might have played a part.

And it seems that people,
going into voluntary lockdown, without
the need of coercive legislation, might have played a part.

And finally,
It seems that people's awareness of social
responsibility, as well as their rights, might have
played a big part.

The Tournament

Under a blazing sun, a gentle breeze,
the odd puff of white cloud plodding its lonely
path over an endless blue sky, the week long
tennis tournament is underway.

It's a chockablock gathering from far and near
of all shapes and sizes, all different ages, players
and watchers, children and dogs, colourful shorts,
colourful tea shirts, baseball caps, panamas and
everything subsumed under a canopy of biffing
and grunting, whooping and sighing,
shouting and laughing.

It seems the pandemic is now stored away in the
wardrobe of memory, at least for the time being and
replaced more immediately by the sliced backhand,
the blistering serve, the overhead smash and
the carefully disguised lob.

Cars fill the surrounding roads and
refreshments flow from the clubhouse to
jolly groups gathered, waiting, mingling
and shifting outside
and all in all
it's a festive occasion if ever there was one.

A news headline yesterday said:
"Lockdown solidarity is starting to fray."
One has to ponder,
I wonder what gives them that idea?

Retired

She said: I've just heard Palmerston's retired.
He said: Palmerston?
She said: Yes he's retired.
He said: Palmerston's dead. Died in 1865.
She said: No, Palmerston. The foreign office cat.
He said: Oh that Palmerston. He hasn't got Covid?
She said: No, apparently he's had enough. Fed up with catching mice I suppose.
He said: Where's he going to?
She said: I don't know. Probably some exclusive sanctuary in the Bahamas or Cayman islands. Probably got a stash of expensive cat food out there.

Exam Results

From a vantage point high
above the educational tundra
one has observed for many weeks
the predictable and clearly defined
outline of a dog waiting for its dinner.

A Memory Repeated

In a time long passed one recalls an ill-considered
but innocent venture onto a noon day Singapore street
that found, lying in wait, an inconsiderate, unyielding,
almost touchable wall of heat that then folded around,
wrapped around, encircled and cocooned the unweary,
unsuspecting, gullible tourist.

The attempt which followed to advance a few
hundred meters soon found the same unfortunate
and luckless creature gasping for breath, drenched
in sweat, and beating a Napoleonic Moscow style
retreat back to the safety of the airconditioned hotel.

One thought
an experience never to be repeated here in Blighty
but a few days ago, venturing from house to garden,
there it was albeit less severe but nevertheless a
memory reignited and reproduced in Walmer.

Good heavens whatever next?

Foreign Climes

(On the telephone)

1st Man:	Oh, you're back then. Have a good time?
2nd Man:	Yeah not bad. Very hot down there though and, of course, now we've got to put up with all this quarantine nonsense!
1st Man:	Well just for this year you might have been better off staying at home. Maybe gone to Clacton? After all you've been on furlough for the last four months.
2nd Man:	Oh no, we always go to the South of France. I don't see why we should change and anyway who wants to go to Clacton?
1st Man:	What's wrong with Clacton?

The Recreation Ground

Passing the recreation ground and for a
moment stopping to watch a game of football,
with no restrictions or social distancing,
suddenly through the mists of time it's me
and suddenly, seeping into view, all my old team
mates in spectral form on a cold miserable day.
And I can see
Bobby with silky skills, Billy with crunching tackles,
Alan with his fierce shot, Peter getting stuck in,
Brian on the wing and Chris, rangy and fleet of foot
galloping into the penalty area to smash the ball into
the waiting and impartial, no longer empty, net.

And I can see
a segment or two of orange at half time, someone
remembered to bring them, and then the resumption
with lots of shouting, goal line clearances, slide rule passes,
fingertip saves and all in the freezing icy cold
winds of a soaking Flanders filled muddy Saturday afternoon.
And I can see:
a hot shower at the final whistle, if you were quick,
it soon went cold, soon went to a struggling dribble.
Not funny if covered and caked in layered mud.
Then I can see
a brief argument with the 'jobs worth' council employed
groundsman who tried to stop us playing in the first place,
and then it was all over. Homeward bound.
The end of an action packed thoroughly enjoyable day
but only because we won.
All this I can see now
and maybe replicated in the years that are left
and maybe replicated forever.

On the Plus Side

In the East End, harping back to the 1950's, but
not with rose tinted glasses,
one remembers, grownups, men and women,
sometimes saying: "I had a good war."
And puzzling, because I knew about the bombs,
saw the bomb sites, knew about people dying,
knew about lots of people dying.
And later, more in adolescence, one learned of
the challenges, adventures and comradeship that
bound people together and the loosening of moral
constraints that released a chance to 'have a good war'
It was an experience buried by some but relived
and replayed by others, over and over again, for the
rest of their nostalgic lives.

One wonders now, in years to come, if people,
some people, will say they 'had a good Covid.'
Most notably being furloughed for an all expenses
paid, once in a lifetime, seven-month excursion to
dreamland. Given money to do it.
Not real money, of course, not earned, 'Toy-Town'
money, pseudo money to go on trips, lay on the
beach, barbecues, tennis, cycling and so on and so on
and so on, all in a blazing hot endless summer.
And for the children, four months and no school.
Surely something to remember in years to come
and surely disgraceful. *Disgraceful I missed it.*

But it's often remarked and it's true I'm sure that
nothing in life is free. There's always a price to be paid
and perhaps later, in the autumn, after October 31st
with the buffers in place, ready and waiting,
reality dawns.

Maybe

Maybe at some point, peering into the haze,
following this spiteful, all enveloping storm and in a
tranquil reflective interlude there's an opportunity,
a chance to reassess, to refocus, to rebalance.

And maybe in the 'pending' tray of 'maybe'
to put more emphasis on 'Us' and less on 'Me'
Globally, nationally individually,
to rediscover neglected, half forgotten, musty
values to do with altruism, to do with consensus,
to do with community, to do with compassion.
All still there. All patiently waiting to be released,
for the key to be turned, to be unlocked.

And maybe there's a chance to rebalance productively
More emphasis on making things, sustainably,
ecologically, usefully; to be productive usefully.
Less emphasis on property, on buying and
selling houses, on renting and collecting houses,
(for those who can afford them)
A chance to move away from the giant
all absorbing warehouse known as GB Inc and
its obsessive consumption of planned obsolescence.
Away from acquisition for its own sake.

And maybe after the vaccine,
after the increased survival rate,
overhanging all the maybe mentioned so far,
is the item marked and underlined for all to see
Global Warming.

Climate change must be on top of the tray.
So lots of possibilities and there is a chance
for rebirth, to start again, to start afresh.
Maybe.

Locked out in Lockdown

At 10.30 pm my wife retired to bed leaving yours truly in the conservatory playing patience and listening to the radio.
An hour later I also decided to retire after listening to various world leaders prognosticate on various aspects of the Covid 19 crisis; all guaranteed to give someone a good night's kip. So now attempting to open the door connecting the conservatory to the rest of the house, the reader can only imagine my dismay and alarm at finding that my wife in a moment of absent mindedness, I'm not a conspiracy theorist, had locked me out. Hence…

I was now isolated from the rest of the house. No chance of cries of 'Help' being heard as our bedroom is upstairs at the front of a large Victorian building. So, after a moment or two's panic I managed to regroup and calmly reflect on my limited options, which boiled down to spending an uncomfortable night in the conservatory or attempting some form of escape. Not exactly on the Stalag 17 scale, but considering the keys, linking the conservatory to the garden, were also inside the house and beyond reach, it certainly presented me with something of a challenge.

Climbing through the conservatory window into a heavy drizzle my first course of action was to procure a ladder from the garage. The plan being to climb onto the garage roof and then pull the ladder up behind me which I could then lower onto the service road at the rear of the garage and effect my escape. Sounds simple enough, but easier said than done, because you now have a seventy-six-year-old man in his bedroom slippers - in the drizzle - standing on an asbestos roof that's at least fifty years old and covered in verdigris, with nothing to hold on to and making his way with the ladder across the roof to lower it onto the street. A feat akin to walking a tight rope in the dark, at midnight, with the real possibility of falling off or in this case going through the roof. Nerve racking to say the least.

After alighting on to the street, fortunately there was no one around, I made my way about two hundred and fifty meters round the block, to the front of the house, where I attempted to raise the alarm by ringing the doorbell. Once again it sounds simple enough but after five minutes or so of numerous unrequited attempts of jamming my finger against the door bell and no sigh of life, things were starting to look desperate.

The options now were firstly to throw stones at the bedroom window or secondly to shout loudly and hope that either action would cause my wife to emerge from her comatose state. The first possible course of action was discounted on the grounds that stones might damage recently installed double glazing and thus add to my misfortune in a pecuniary fashion while the second was eliminated with the realisation that to have any effect the volume of noise would need to be considerable and thus more likely attract ridicule and possible annoyance from those in the adjacent houses. The image of a, by now, soaked neighbour standing in the street in bedroom slippers at 12.30 am in the morning, was too much to bear. One has one's pride.

In the end I decided on a third option which was to walk back round to the rear of the house and carry the ladder round to the front. I could then place it against the porch roof which lies just below the bedroom window and thus, hopefully, rouse my wife and precipitate entry to the house.

The reader will now be pleased to learn that this went smoothly, thank God no one came along, and I rapped firmly on the bedroom window and managed to rouse my wife from her slumbers. She then looked grumpily through the bedroom window and said: "What are you doing out there?" An alternative answer was to inform her that I was just checking the porch roof for any possible leaks but in the end I just said: "You locked me out." So, the conclusion to this bizarre and eventful episode was that I gained entry to the house but was at the same time reprimanded for depositing mud on the hall-carpet.

Authors Note

Dear readers,

Given the circumstances and subject matter I hesitate to say: "I hope you enjoyed the book" but hopefully it has provided and will continue to provide some slight diversion, until this unique period in our lives has passed and we can return to a more 'normal and predictable routine.' Always, at the same time, being aware that a 'normal and predictable routine' may well have undergone some degree of redefinition. In the meantime take care and stay safe.

Best wishes

Ted Roche

NB As usual any monies accruing will go to charity. Watch out for *Nuffink in Particular Part 3* in 2021.

INDEX OF TITLES AND FIRST LINES

Titles are in *italic*. If the first line is the same as the title, then only the first line will be written.

Louannvee Publishing
www.louannveepublishing.co.uk

Printed in Poland
by Amazon Fulfillment
Poland Sp. z o.o., Wrocław

65560750R00040